Treasures of the Sea
BIRTHDAY BOOK

THIS BOOK BELONGS TO:

_____
NAME

_____
ADDRESS

_____
TELEPHONE

_____
EMAIL

PERSONAL DETAILS

NAME

ADDRESS

TELEPHONE

FAX   MOBILE

EMAIL

IN CASE OF EMERGENCY

CONTACT

TELEPHONE

BLOOD GROUP

KNOWN ALLERGIES

USEFUL INFORMATION

HEALTH INSURANCE NO.

PASSPORT NO.

DRIVERS LICENCE

CREDIT CARDS

OTHER DETAILS

STAR SIGNS

AQUARIUS
(January 21 - February 19)
Sensitive, stubborn, independent, lovable,
unpredictable, funny

PISCES
(February 20 - March 20)
Sweet, charming, fanciful, non-conformist, artistic, wise

ARIES
(March 21 - April 20)
Strong, active, affectionate, determined

TAURUS
(April 21 - May 20)
Calm, pleasant, cheerful, stubborn, artistic

GEMINI
(May 21 - June 21)
Bright, friendly, clever, humorous, imaginative

CANCER
(June 22 - July 23)
Sensitive, artistic, funny, temperamental, loving

LEO
(July 24 - August 23)
Light-hearted, active, extroverted, strong-willed

VIRGO
(August 24 - September 23)
Calm, alert, companionable, dependable

LIBRA
(September 24 - October 23)
Quiet, calm, well-mannered, kind-hearted, cautious

SCORPIO
(October 24 - November 22)
Wise, brave, loyal, determined

SAGITTARIUS
(November 23 - December 22)
Happy, light-hearted, curious, independent

CAPRICORN
(December 23 - January 20)
Strong-willed, purposeful, bright, artistic

JANUARY

NAME

BIRTH DATE   STAR SIGN

GIFT SUGGESTIONS

NAME

BIRTH DATE   STAR SIGN

GIFT SUGGESTIONS

NAME

BIRTH DATE   STAR SIGN

GIFT SUGGESTIONS

NAME

BIRTH DATE   STAR SIGN

GIFT SUGGESTIONS

NAME

BIRTH DATE   STAR SIGN

GIFT SUGGESTIONS

JANUARY

NAME _____

BIRTH DATE _____ STAR SIGN _____

GIFT SUGGESTIONS _____

NAME _____

BIRTH DATE _____ STAR SIGN _____

GIFT SUGGESTIONS _____

NAME _____

BIRTH DATE _____ STAR SIGN _____

GIFT SUGGESTIONS _____

NAME _____

BIRTH DATE _____ STAR SIGN _____

GIFT SUGGESTIONS _____

NAME _____

BIRTH DATE _____ STAR SIGN _____

GIFT SUGGESTIONS _____

NAME

BIRTH DATE   STAR SIGN

GIFT SUGGESTIONS

NAME

BIRTH DATE   STAR SIGN

GIFT SUGGESTIONS

NAME

BIRTH DATE   STAR SIGN

GIFT SUGGESTIONS

NAME

BIRTH DATE   STAR SIGN

GIFT SUGGESTIONS

NAME

BIRTH DATE   STAR SIGN

GIFT SUGGESTIONS

FEBRUARY

NAME

BIRTH DATE   STAR SIGN

GIFT SUGGESTIONS

NAME

BIRTH DATE   STAR SIGN

GIFT SUGGESTIONS

NAME

BIRTH DATE   STAR SIGN

GIFT SUGGESTIONS

NAME

BIRTH DATE   STAR SIGN

GIFT SUGGESTIONS

NAME

BIRTH DATE   STAR SIGN

GIFT SUGGESTIONS

FEBRUARY

NAME

BIRTH DATE   STAR SIGN

GIFT SUGGESTIONS

NAME

BIRTH DATE   STAR SIGN

GIFT SUGGESTIONS

NAME

BIRTH DATE   STAR SIGN

GIFT SUGGESTIONS

NAME

BIRTH DATE   STAR SIGN

GIFT SUGGESTIONS

NAME

BIRTH DATE   STAR SIGN

GIFT SUGGESTIONS

NAME

BIRTH DATE   STAR SIGN

GIFT SUGGESTIONS

NAME

BIRTH DATE   STAR SIGN

GIFT SUGGESTIONS

NAME

BIRTH DATE   STAR SIGN

GIFT SUGGESTIONS

NAME

BIRTH DATE   STAR SIGN

GIFT SUGGESTIONS

NAME

BIRTH DATE   STAR SIGN

GIFT SUGGESTIONS

MARCH

NAME _____

BIRTH DATE _____ STAR SIGN _____

GIFT SUGGESTIONS _____

NAME _____

BIRTH DATE _____ STAR SIGN _____

GIFT SUGGESTIONS _____

NAME _____

BIRTH DATE _____ STAR SIGN _____

GIFT SUGGESTIONS _____

NAME _____

BIRTH DATE _____ STAR SIGN _____

GIFT SUGGESTIONS _____

NAME _____

BIRTH DATE _____ STAR SIGN _____

GIFT SUGGESTIONS _____

MARCH

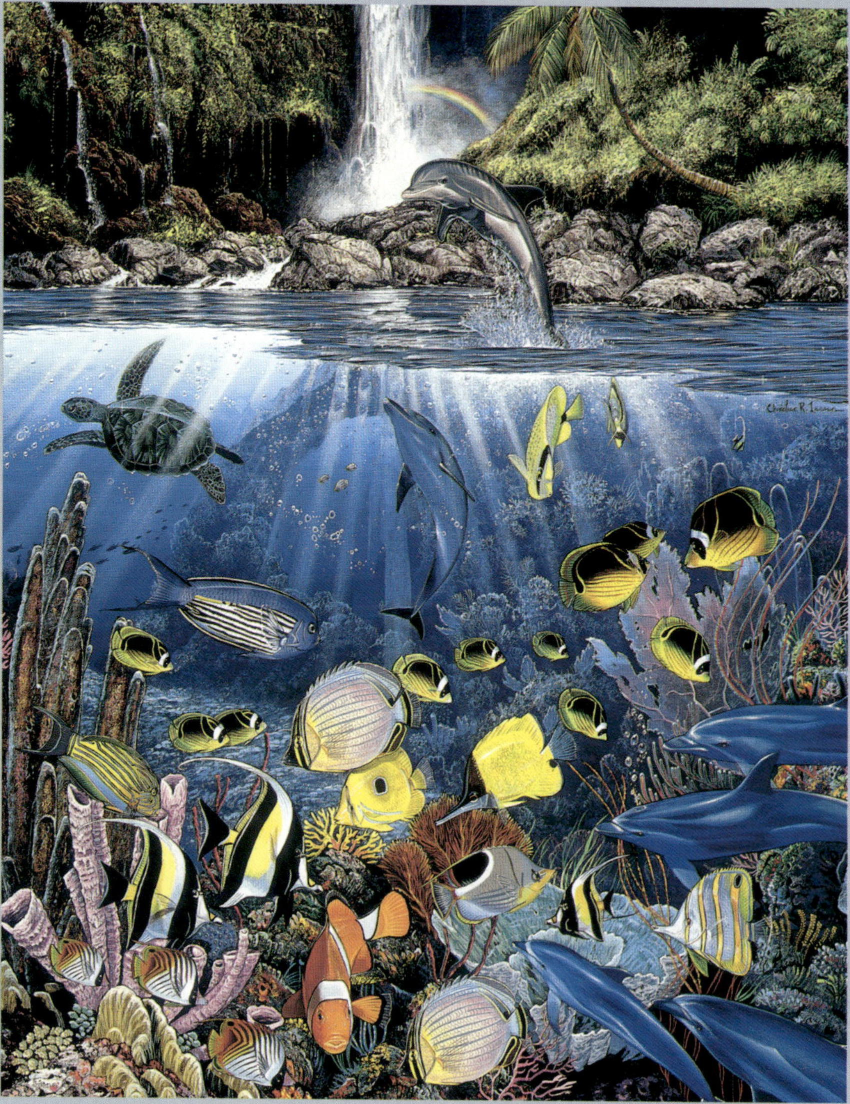

MARCH

NAME

BIRTH DATE   STAR SIGN

GIFT SUGGESTIONS

NAME

BIRTH DATE   STAR SIGN

GIFT SUGGESTIONS

NAME

BIRTH DATE   STAR SIGN

GIFT SUGGESTIONS

NAME

BIRTH DATE   STAR SIGN

GIFT SUGGESTIONS

NAME

BIRTH DATE   STAR SIGN

GIFT SUGGESTIONS

NAME _____

BIRTH DATE _____ STAR SIGN _____

GIFT SUGGESTIONS _____

NAME _____

BIRTH DATE _____ STAR SIGN _____

GIFT SUGGESTIONS _____

NAME _____

BIRTH DATE _____ STAR SIGN _____

GIFT SUGGESTIONS _____

NAME _____

BIRTH DATE _____ STAR SIGN _____

GIFT SUGGESTIONS _____

NAME _____

BIRTH DATE _____ STAR SIGN _____

GIFT SUGGESTIONS _____

APRIL

NAME _____

BIRTH DATE _____ STAR SIGN _____

GIFT SUGGESTIONS _____

NAME _____

BIRTH DATE _____ STAR SIGN _____

GIFT SUGGESTIONS _____

NAME _____

BIRTH DATE _____ STAR SIGN _____

GIFT SUGGESTIONS _____

NAME _____

BIRTH DATE _____ STAR SIGN _____

GIFT SUGGESTIONS _____

NAME _____

BIRTH DATE _____ STAR SIGN _____

GIFT SUGGESTIONS _____

Larsen

APRIL

NAME

BIRTH DATE   STAR SIGN

GIFT SUGGESTIONS

NAME

BIRTH DATE   STAR SIGN

GIFT SUGGESTIONS

NAME

BIRTH DATE   STAR SIGN

GIFT SUGGESTIONS

NAME

BIRTH DATE   STAR SIGN

GIFT SUGGESTIONS

NAME

BIRTH DATE   STAR SIGN

GIFT SUGGESTIONS

NAME

BIRTH DATE   STAR SIGN

GIFT SUGGESTIONS

NAME

BIRTH DATE   STAR SIGN

GIFT SUGGESTIONS

NAME

BIRTH DATE   STAR SIGN

GIFT SUGGESTIONS

NAME

BIRTH DATE   STAR SIGN

GIFT SUGGESTIONS

NAME

BIRTH DATE   STAR SIGN

GIFT SUGGESTIONS

MAY

NAME

BIRTH DATE   STAR SIGN

GIFT SUGGESTIONS

NAME

BIRTH DATE   STAR SIGN

GIFT SUGGESTIONS

NAME

BIRTH DATE   STAR SIGN

GIFT SUGGESTIONS

NAME

BIRTH DATE   STAR SIGN

GIFT SUGGESTIONS

NAME

BIRTH DATE   STAR SIGN

GIFT SUGGESTIONS

MAY

NAME

BIRTH DATE   STAR SIGN

GIFT SUGGESTIONS

NAME

BIRTH DATE   STAR SIGN

GIFT SUGGESTIONS

NAME

BIRTH DATE   STAR SIGN

GIFT SUGGESTIONS

NAME

BIRTH DATE   STAR SIGN

GIFT SUGGESTIONS

NAME

BIRTH DATE   STAR SIGN

GIFT SUGGESTIONS

NAME

BIRTH DATE   STAR SIGN

GIFT SUGGESTIONS

NAME

BIRTH DATE   STAR SIGN

GIFT SUGGESTIONS

NAME

BIRTH DATE   STAR SIGN

GIFT SUGGESTIONS

NAME

BIRTH DATE   STAR SIGN

GIFT SUGGESTIONS

NAME

BIRTH DATE   STAR SIGN

GIFT SUGGESTIONS

JUNE

NAME

BIRTH DATE   STAR SIGN

GIFT SUGGESTIONS

NAME

BIRTH DATE   STAR SIGN

GIFT SUGGESTIONS

NAME

BIRTH DATE   STAR SIGN

GIFT SUGGESTIONS

NAME

BIRTH DATE   STAR SIGN

GIFT SUGGESTIONS

NAME

BIRTH DATE   STAR SIGN

GIFT SUGGESTIONS

JUNE

NAME _____

BIRTH DATE _____ STAR SIGN _____

GIFT SUGGESTIONS _____

NAME _____

BIRTH DATE _____ STAR SIGN _____

GIFT SUGGESTIONS _____

NAME _____

BIRTH DATE _____ STAR SIGN _____

GIFT SUGGESTIONS _____

NAME _____

BIRTH DATE _____ STAR SIGN _____

GIFT SUGGESTIONS _____

NAME _____

BIRTH DATE _____ STAR SIGN _____

GIFT SUGGESTIONS _____

NAME

BIRTH DATE   STAR SIGN

GIFT SUGGESTIONS

NAME

BIRTH DATE   STAR SIGN

GIFT SUGGESTIONS

NAME

BIRTH DATE   STAR SIGN

GIFT SUGGESTIONS

NAME

BIRTH DATE   STAR SIGN

GIFT SUGGESTIONS

NAME

BIRTH DATE   STAR SIGN

GIFT SUGGESTIONS

JULY

NAME

BIRTH DATE   STAR SIGN

GIFT SUGGESTIONS

NAME

BIRTH DATE   STAR SIGN

GIFT SUGGESTIONS

NAME

BIRTH DATE   STAR SIGN

GIFT SUGGESTIONS

NAME

BIRTH DATE   STAR SIGN

GIFT SUGGESTIONS

NAME

BIRTH DATE   STAR SIGN

GIFT SUGGESTIONS

JULY

NAME

BIRTH DATE   STAR SIGN

GIFT SUGGESTIONS

NAME

BIRTH DATE   STAR SIGN

GIFT SUGGESTIONS

NAME

BIRTH DATE   STAR SIGN

GIFT SUGGESTIONS

NAME

BIRTH DATE   STAR SIGN

GIFT SUGGESTIONS

NAME

BIRTH DATE   STAR SIGN

GIFT SUGGESTIONS

NAME _____

BIRTH DATE _____ STAR SIGN _____

GIFT SUGGESTIONS _____

NAME _____

BIRTH DATE _____ STAR SIGN _____

GIFT SUGGESTIONS _____

NAME _____

BIRTH DATE _____ STAR SIGN _____

GIFT SUGGESTIONS _____

NAME _____

BIRTH DATE _____ STAR SIGN _____

GIFT SUGGESTIONS _____

NAME _____

BIRTH DATE _____ STAR SIGN _____

GIFT SUGGESTIONS _____

AUGUST

NAME
_____

BIRTH DATE
_____   STAR SIGN
_____

GIFT SUGGESTIONS
_____

NAME
_____

BIRTH DATE
_____   STAR SIGN
_____

GIFT SUGGESTIONS
_____

NAME
_____

BIRTH DATE
_____   STAR SIGN
_____

GIFT SUGGESTIONS
_____

NAME
_____

BIRTH DATE
_____   STAR SIGN
_____

GIFT SUGGESTIONS
_____

NAME
_____

BIRTH DATE
_____   STAR SIGN
_____

GIFT SUGGESTIONS
_____

AUGUST

NAME

BIRTH DATE   STAR SIGN

GIFT SUGGESTIONS

NAME

BIRTH DATE   STAR SIGN

GIFT SUGGESTIONS

NAME

BIRTH DATE   STAR SIGN

GIFT SUGGESTIONS

NAME

BIRTH DATE   STAR SIGN

GIFT SUGGESTIONS

NAME

BIRTH DATE   STAR SIGN

GIFT SUGGESTIONS

NAME _____

BIRTH DATE _____ STAR SIGN _____

GIFT SUGGESTIONS _____

NAME _____

BIRTH DATE _____ STAR SIGN _____

GIFT SUGGESTIONS _____

NAME _____

BIRTH DATE _____ STAR SIGN _____

GIFT SUGGESTIONS _____

NAME _____

BIRTH DATE _____ STAR SIGN _____

GIFT SUGGESTIONS _____

NAME _____

BIRTH DATE _____ STAR SIGN _____

GIFT SUGGESTIONS _____

SEPTEMBER

NAME _____

BIRTH DATE _____ STAR SIGN _____

GIFT SUGGESTIONS _____

NAME _____

BIRTH DATE _____ STAR SIGN _____

GIFT SUGGESTIONS _____

NAME _____

BIRTH DATE _____ STAR SIGN _____

GIFT SUGGESTIONS _____

NAME _____

BIRTH DATE _____ STAR SIGN _____

GIFT SUGGESTIONS _____

NAME _____

BIRTH DATE _____ STAR SIGN _____

GIFT SUGGESTIONS _____

SEPTEMBER

NAME

BIRTH DATE   STAR SIGN

GIFT SUGGESTIONS

NAME

BIRTH DATE   STAR SIGN

GIFT SUGGESTIONS

NAME

BIRTH DATE   STAR SIGN

GIFT SUGGESTIONS

NAME

BIRTH DATE   STAR SIGN

GIFT SUGGESTIONS

NAME

BIRTH DATE   STAR SIGN

GIFT SUGGESTIONS

NAME

BIRTH DATE   STAR SIGN

GIFT SUGGESTIONS

NAME

BIRTH DATE   STAR SIGN

GIFT SUGGESTIONS

NAME

BIRTH DATE   STAR SIGN

GIFT SUGGESTIONS

NAME

BIRTH DATE   STAR SIGN

GIFT SUGGESTIONS

NAME

BIRTH DATE   STAR SIGN

GIFT SUGGESTIONS

OCTOBER

NAME

BIRTH DATE   STAR SIGN

GIFT SUGGESTIONS

NAME

BIRTH DATE   STAR SIGN

GIFT SUGGESTIONS

NAME

BIRTH DATE   STAR SIGN

GIFT SUGGESTIONS

NAME

BIRTH DATE   STAR SIGN

GIFT SUGGESTIONS

NAME

BIRTH DATE   STAR SIGN

GIFT SUGGESTIONS

OCTOBER

NAME

BIRTH DATE   STAR SIGN

GIFT SUGGESTIONS

NAME

BIRTH DATE   STAR SIGN

GIFT SUGGESTIONS

NAME

BIRTH DATE   STAR SIGN

GIFT SUGGESTIONS

NAME

BIRTH DATE   STAR SIGN

GIFT SUGGESTIONS

NAME

BIRTH DATE   STAR SIGN

GIFT SUGGESTIONS

NAME _____

BIRTH DATE _____ STAR SIGN _____

GIFT SUGGESTIONS _____

NAME _____

BIRTH DATE _____ STAR SIGN _____

GIFT SUGGESTIONS _____

NAME _____

BIRTH DATE _____ STAR SIGN _____

GIFT SUGGESTIONS _____

NAME _____

BIRTH DATE _____ STAR SIGN _____

GIFT SUGGESTIONS _____

NAME _____

BIRTH DATE _____ STAR SIGN _____

GIFT SUGGESTIONS _____

NOVEMBER

NAME

BIRTH DATE   STAR SIGN

GIFT SUGGESTIONS

NAME

BIRTH DATE   STAR SIGN

GIFT SUGGESTIONS

NAME

BIRTH DATE   STAR SIGN

GIFT SUGGESTIONS

NAME

BIRTH DATE   STAR SIGN

GIFT SUGGESTIONS

NAME

BIRTH DATE   STAR SIGN

GIFT SUGGESTIONS

NOVEMBER

NAME _____

BIRTH DATE _____ STAR SIGN _____

GIFT SUGGESTIONS _____

NAME _____

BIRTH DATE _____ STAR SIGN _____

GIFT SUGGESTIONS _____

NAME _____

BIRTH DATE _____ STAR SIGN _____

GIFT SUGGESTIONS _____

NAME _____

BIRTH DATE _____ STAR SIGN _____

GIFT SUGGESTIONS _____

NAME _____

BIRTH DATE _____ STAR SIGN _____

GIFT SUGGESTIONS _____

NAME

BIRTH DATE   STAR SIGN

GIFT SUGGESTIONS

NAME

BIRTH DATE   STAR SIGN

GIFT SUGGESTIONS

NAME

BIRTH DATE   STAR SIGN

GIFT SUGGESTIONS

NAME

BIRTH DATE   STAR SIGN

GIFT SUGGESTIONS

NAME

BIRTH DATE   STAR SIGN

GIFT SUGGESTIONS

DECEMBER

NAME

BIRTH DATE   STAR SIGN

GIFT SUGGESTIONS

NAME

BIRTH DATE   STAR SIGN

GIFT SUGGESTIONS

NAME

BIRTH DATE   STAR SIGN

GIFT SUGGESTIONS

NAME

BIRTH DATE   STAR SIGN

GIFT SUGGESTIONS

NAME

BIRTH DATE   STAR SIGN

GIFT SUGGESTIONS

DECEMBER

NAME

BIRTH DATE   STAR SIGN

GIFT SUGGESTIONS

NAME

BIRTH DATE   STAR SIGN

GIFT SUGGESTIONS

NAME

BIRTH DATE   STAR SIGN

GIFT SUGGESTIONS

NAME

BIRTH DATE   STAR SIGN

GIFT SUGGESTIONS

NAME

BIRTH DATE   STAR SIGN

GIFT SUGGESTIONS

NAME

BIRTH DATE   STAR SIGN

GIFT SUGGESTIONS

NAME

BIRTH DATE   STAR SIGN

GIFT SUGGESTIONS

NAME

BIRTH DATE   STAR SIGN

GIFT SUGGESTIONS

NAME

BIRTH DATE   STAR SIGN

GIFT SUGGESTIONS

NAME

BIRTH DATE   STAR SIGN

GIFT SUGGESTIONS

BIRTH FLOWERS

January	Snowdrop for purity
February	Carnation for courage
March	Violet for modesty
April	Lily for virtue
May	Hawthorn for hope
June	Rose for beauty
July	Daisy for innocence
August	Poppy for peace
September	Morning Glory for contentment
October	Cosmos for aspirations
November	Chrysanthemum for cheerfulness
December	Holly for foresight

BIRTHSTONES

January	Garnet for constancy
February	Amethyst for sincerity
March	Aquamarine for courage
April	Diamond for innocence
May	Emerald for tranquillity
June	Pearl for purity
July	Ruby for nobility
August	Moonstone for joy
September	Sapphire for wisdom
October	Opal for hope
November	Topaz for loyalty
December	Turquoise for success

WEDDING ANNIVERSARIES

COUPLE'S NAMES _____

ANNIVERSARY DATE _____

GIFT SUGGESTIONS _____

COUPLE'S NAMES _____

ANNIVERSARY DATE _____

GIFT SUGGESTIONS _____

COUPLE'S NAMES _____

ANNIVERSARY DATE _____

GIFT SUGGESTIONS _____

COUPLE'S NAMES _____

ANNIVERSARY DATE _____

GIFT SUGGESTIONS _____

COUPLE'S NAMES _____

ANNIVERSARY DATE _____

GIFT SUGGESTIONS _____

COUPLE'S NAMES _____

ANNIVERSARY DATE _____

GIFT SUGGESTIONS _____

COUPLE'S NAMES _____

ANNIVERSARY DATE _____

GIFT SUGGESTIONS _____

COUPLE'S NAMES _____

ANNIVERSARY DATE _____

GIFT SUGGESTIONS _____

COUPLE'S NAMES _____

ANNIVERSARY DATE _____

GIFT SUGGESTIONS _____

COUPLE'S NAMES _____

ANNIVERSARY DATE _____

GIFT SUGGESTIONS _____

COUPLE'S NAMES _____

ANNIVERSARY DATE _____

GIFT SUGGESTIONS _____

COUPLE'S NAMES _____

ANNIVERSARY DATE _____

GIFT SUGGESTIONS _____

SPECIAL OCCASIONS

NAME _____ DATE _____

OCCASION _____

NAME _____ DATE _____

OCCASION _____

NAME _____ DATE _____

OCCASION _____

NAME _____ DATE _____

OCCASION _____

NAME _____ DATE _____

OCCASION _____

NAME _____ DATE _____

OCCASION _____

NAME _____ DATE _____

OCCASION _____

NAME _____ DATE _____

OCCASION _____

NAME _____ DATE _____

OCCASION _____

NAME   DATE
_____   _____

OCCASION
_____

NAME   DATE
_____   _____

OCCASION
_____

NAME   DATE
_____   _____

OCCASION
_____

NAME   DATE
_____   _____

OCCASION
_____

NAME   DATE
_____   _____

OCCASION
_____

NAME   DATE
_____   _____

OCCASION
_____

NAME   DATE
_____   _____

OCCASION
_____

NAME   DATE
_____   _____

OCCASION
_____

NAME   DATE
_____   _____

OCCASION
_____

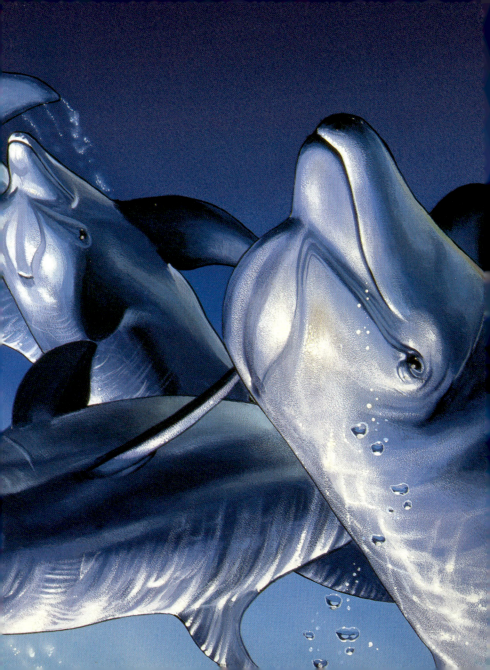